Blessings,
Gifts & Deeds

Bless Your Heart

Blessings,
Gifts & Deeds

This entire book plus
interviews & background
information is available on
the Internet at:

http://www.artxpo.com/XTRA/blessings/blessings.html

Blessings,
Gifts & Deeds

Building your celestial mansion

Joseph Crane

WEST COAST
Media
G R O U P

WEST COAST
Media
G R O U P

P.O. Box 8245
Emeryville, California 94662

West Coast Media Group is a division of TQS Publications.

Library of Congress Cataloging-in-Publication Data

Crane. Joseph, 1946-
    Blessings, gifts & deeds : building your celestial mansion /
Joseph Crane.
       p.   cm.
    ISBN 0-89229-037-4 (pb)
    1. Crane, Joseph, 1946- . 2. Spiritual biography--United
States. 3. Michael (Archangel)--Miscellanea. 4. Spiritual life.
I. Title.
BL73.C73A3 1996   96-30398
291.4--dc20   CIP

First printing: September 1996

To my two best friends
Tony (Chico) Chavez, who went home in 1992,
and my father who went home in 1989. Your
counsel will be sorely missed and yet you really
know of what I write.

Acknowledgments

I'd like to give my thanks to the following: To the angel Michael for giving me this to do. To my wife, Donna, for all she has given and done to get this book written. To Bud, Barb, Richard and Chris for giving me the wife I have. To Poppy, Baron, Bogie and Annie, my dogs that let me know the angel was OK.

To Alexander Everett for his teachings and counsel. To Deb, Kathleen and Mark for knowing who they are.

To my friends and family in appreciation for all they have done in helping me finish this book: Al Coppala, Gregory Clark and his sister Patricia Clark, Bill and Chris Godbey, Christina and Rob Grooms, Terry and his family, my mother and my cousin Mary.

To Joan Larimore for her assistance in the first edit. To Tyrnie for hooking me up with a publisher. To Branko Romano for his faith in this work and all his assistance in publishing this book.

To you who took the time to read the acknowledgments to the people that made this book possible, bless your heart.

Most of all to a loving God for all of this.

Preface

What you are about to read is a true account of a visitation by an angel. Is it unlike anything you have read? I believe it is, or at least I know for sure *I* haven't read anything like this before. Imagine what it would be like to have an angel appear and bring good news for a change. The last time something like this happened was about two thousand years ago. Again a message is given of God's unconditional love for all. God sees you as perfect, whole and complete just the way you are. A new baptism is given that opens a direct line to God that you may be unaware of. The pages of this book hold the secret of building your mansion in heaven. Within these pages you will find a builder's manual called *The Book of Bricks* which describes the "how-to" in creating your mansion, brick-by-brick.

You will also find this to be, at times, a

humorous journey through a year-long conversation between the angel Michael and me. Michael speaks of things I must do and teach, even though I think he has the wrong man for the job. He talks about seven people that will become <u>Masters</u>. They will teach seven others, who, in turn, will teach seven more, and so on and so on. Open your heart and mind so that your soul will be filled with God's love. Writing this book has opened a relationship with God I never dreamed possible. I only hope that in reading this book, your relationship takes the quantum leap that mine has. Bless your heart.

Table of Contents

CHAPTER 1
Teach Only Love

Christmas is the time when most Christians remember the birth of Jesus. It seems strange that he was born in the spring yet we still celebrate his birth in December. Having been touched by the story of his birth one more time, this year, I decided to read the Bible. Many years had passed since I have had one to read, so I figured it was time to get one. You need to know that this was only for my own knowledge. I'm not a member of any religion. I don't go to church on Sunday, but I do believe in God. I also pray asking for God's guidance and have for many years.

Each night I laid in bed and read the Bible, chapter and verse. I would go over what I had read on the following day. Some of it made sense and some of it did not. After three or four weeks of reading, I asked God to help me understand the real message. The next night I went to bed, took out the Bible, and began reading again.

It was around midnight when I closed my Bible and set it on the night stand. Looking over at my sleeping wife, I thought *what a beautiful woman I married*. I noticed our four mastiffs, two on the bed and the others on the floor. "Whatever have I done to be so blessed with such a lovely family?" I said to myself, as I reached over to turn off the light and kiss Donna good night.

Putting my head on the pillow, I settled in, pulling the covers over my shoulders. Feeling the warmth of the waterbed relax my body I slowly began drifting off to that place where we go just before sleep, when our minds are clear of all thought.

"**Joe**," a voice said. "**Joe**," the voice said again. I was now fully awake trying to decide what course of action to take, for this was not the first time something like this had happened to me. On three other occasions, as far back as ten years ago, I had heard this voice. I always thought it was my roommate calling, but each time when I woke them to ask what they wanted, they told me that they hadn't called me. Once I was home alone when I heard my name called. I got out of bed and went to the door thinking it was someone outside, but no one was there.

I told my friend, Alexander Everett, about my experiences and he asked me if I was familiar with the story of Samuel. I had heard the story before but could not remember any specifics.

Samuel was in the spiritual tutoring of a master named Eli. One night Samuel went to bed and before dawn he heard a voice call **"Samuel! Samuel!"** So he got up, went to Eli, and asked him what he wanted. Eli told him, "I didn't call you, go back to bed." Samuel did so, but again he heard, **"Samuel! Samuel!"** So off to Eli he went, only to be told, "I didn't call you! Go back to bed." The third time he heard **"Samuel! Samuel!"**, he went to Eli and said, "Here I am, for you called me." Eli realized that the Lord must be the one calling Samuel. Eli instructed

Samuel to go back to bed and told him if he was called again to say, "Speak Lord, for your servant hears." Samuel did what he was told and the Lord spoke to him.

"So Joe," Alexander said, "the next time you hear your name called, say, 'Speak Lord, for your servant hears' and see what happens. God just may have something to say to you."

By this time I had serious doubts. *Oh sure*, I thought, *with all the people in the world to talk to, God is going to talk to me. Why me? What does he want from me? I really hope it is not that I'm supposed to do something. Maybe I am just hearing things, or maybe I'm going crazy.*

O.K., I thought, *let's go for it, what's the worst that could happen? I might feel like a fool and then I'll go to sleep and forget all about it by morning.* So I said, "Speak, Lord, for your servant hears." There was no reply.

I saw a pinpoint of light in the doorway, it looked like a piece of glitter on black velvet hit by blinding white light. It began to grow. *Oh boy,* I thought, *I'm in big trouble now. Why did I ever start this?* The light was beginning to fill the doorway. As it did, it was becoming a bright, yet soft, blue-white and spilled onto the walls, illuminating the room.

If this is a dream, I thought, *then the dogs are having it too because each one has his head up looking in the same direction that I am.* I guess it must be O.K., or at least seven hundred pounds of muscle, teeth and loyalty seem to think so. If the dogs aren't afraid, I'm not either... not much, anyway.

Maybe if I just sit still, whatever it is

won't see me, I thought. Better yet, if I just pull the covers over my head, it won't find me and will go away. I didn't do either one. I just sat there with my mouth open, waiting to see what would happen next. I looked over to see if the dogs were going to save me from whatever this was. They weren't.

It looked like someone was coming from far back in the light, moving closer and, yet, already here. At first, the eyes were all I noticed. They were blue, unlike any blue I had ever seen before. *Kind* and *gentle* are the only words to describe those eyes. I felt at peace as I saw the figure more clearly. It had long, platinum blond hair and alabaster skin. Covered in a white robe, it was smiling at us.

The figure spoke in a masculine voice. It struck me as odd that someone so beautiful would appear to be male. **"Put down your books for they hold no truth for you."** he said. **"As the sands of the desert have been moved to suit the winds of time, so has the light been darkened by man's ink on the pages.**

"This you must do or you will not be called upon again. Teach this which Lord God has charged me to give you, for it is the last baptism of God's children. Have those you teach, in turn teach others, for they are well-meaning in their houses of God. You are not a Christ or even a prophet, but a servant of God (who will put words in your mouth) and God's children will hear and understand.

"Take a jug of wine before sunrise and pour it into a bowl. Set this bowl in the sun's path so the light will warm it. Fast, and be still until the sun is at its highest place in the sky.

At this time, go to where the bowl has been laid on the ground and remove your shoes, for you stand on holy ground. Sit and wash your feet, from your toes to your knees, so that you may stand and walk the earth. Wash your hands from the tips of your fingers to the elbow so you may do God's work. When this is done, kneel and say 'My loving Father, your child has come home to your counsel. Guide me in all things that I must do.' Then take up the bowl of wine and pour it on the ground. As your Mother Earth drinks the unclean liquid, all that is unclean with you, his brothers and sisters, is absolved, just as the blood of God's son was said to do. Go now, be at peace and take care of that which I have given you. Teach only love. After you do this we will speak again."

With that he stepped into the light and faded away as the dogs and I watched. I got out of bed, went to the dining room, pulled out some paper and wrote down what he had told me, word for word. Two days later I told my wife and she asked me what I was going to do. All I could say was, "I don't know. It's not every day an angel comes to me and tells me something this profound, let alone wants me to do and teach this Last Baptism thing."

Why on earth would anyone want to listen to me? It is a good thing the churches don't burn people at the stake anymore, I thought, *at least I don't think they do.*

I called Alexander again to tell him what had taken place and that this was a little frightening to me. Alexander is one of the most spiritual people I have ever met.   I went to a class he was teaching about ten years ago called Inward Bound. I had never seen or met a master before, but from the first moment I saw him I knew he was just that. Over the years I've attended many of his classes and got to know him quite well. If I could talk to anyone about this, it would be him.

Alexander told me that I had had a vision. I knew that, vaguely, but what I really wanted to know was, -- "why me?" It seems to me that there are a lot of people in this world who have a much closer relationship with God than I do. People like Alexander have spent their entire lives teaching spiritual truths. Why didn't the angel go to them? But Alexander told me some people wait all their lives to have such a thing happen. I should be grateful for having been chosen to serve in a grand plan. He also told me

I would most likely hear from the angel again. I KNEW he was going to say that.

He told me that I shouldn't be frightened at what had happened, and to be open to whatever I was told to do by the angel. He asked me to let him know from time to time what was happening. I agreed. It was nice to know that he didn't think I was insane. It was even nicer to know that I didn't think I was insane either. Still, it was no comfort for me to think that I was on some kind of mission from God. So I figured that whatever God wanted me to do, he would give me a sign for when and how to do it.

The next day my door bell rang. There were two nicely dressed people standing there wanting, with all their hearts, to tell me of God's love for me. Was this some kind of a sign or what? *If anyone wanted to listen to my story of the angel*, I thought, *surely it would be someone whose whole life is about God.* I listened to what they had to say about God for awhile and then I proceeded to tell them about what had happened to me. I showed them the baptism I had written down. I felt like a little child giving a gift that was the most special thing in the whole world. I was wrong. By the time these nicely dressed people had left my door, I had been told it was Satan who had come to me, trying to steal my soul and that I would burn in hell forever. My son would grow up to be the Antichrist just like it said in the Bible. Armageddon would be my fault. They didn't want to hear that I have no children, let alone a son. I was crushed by their rejection, almost to the point of tears. How is it that something as beautiful as this could be understood as the work of the devil? So much for whom I thought would listen. The next time I talk to this angel, I vowed to myself, he will have some questions to answer. Which brings me to a second visit, however, it was not the angel I first saw.

I did not rush out the first chance I got to do the baptism. I wanted to think about it before I did anything. While I was thinking about it, I had a visit from someone else. I was lying on the sofa, watching an old movie on the television. Annie, my female mastiff, was sharing the sofa with me, her head resting on my shoulder.

Annie raised her head up and back, as if on the alert. She looked toward the hallway and so did I. Thinking it was Donna, I waited to see her come through the doorway. I saw a light move along the wall as if someone had a flashlight and was coming from the back of the house. *Oh, it must be the angel again*, I thought. A man I had not seen before came out of the hall and stopped just outside of the doorway.

"Who the hell is this?" I said to myself. He stood about six feet tall and he was as thin as a rail. Long white hair surrounded a strong, determined face. A thick bushy set of eyebrows above his deep brown eyes made him look as if he were angry about something. The robe he wore hung down to the floor, with baggy sleeves and a hood. Given the way he dressed and his apparent attitude, he appeared to be a monk, who was quite mad.

Looking at me, he shook his head and walked through the dining room into the kitchen mumbling about something. I looked at Annie and she looked at me as if we were asking each other, "What just happened?" He came out of the kitchen. Still shaking his head as he looked down at the floor, he walked across the dining room and went through the glass patio door which was closed. He stood there shaking his head and talking to himself.

I looked back over at my dog. "Yes indeed," I said to Annie, "This boy is wrapped too tight and crazy as a pet coon with rabies."

The angel never said anything about this. Is this going to be like Dickens where I get visited by three ghosts or what?

Once again, through the glass door he came, and stopped in the middle of the dining room. He looked straight at me and then down at the floor. As he raised his head I could see a calmness had come over him as he started to speak. **"You people have been told from the**

very beginning," he said with a soft slow voice, as if to make sure what he was saying was clear. **"Over the centuries you have been told in a gentle way, so have you been told in a mighty way, of God's love for you. Do you hear it?"** He had a stern voice that got more forceful as he continued to speak without waiting for an answer.

"You people have been given the wonders of the universe, including the world on which you live. Do you say, 'blessed are we? God loves us so much that he gives us all this?' Do you say, 'Brothers and Sisters, we may live long to care for one another? Our happiness and well-being are great with God?' NO." He said in a resounding voice that almost shook the room. **"You people would rather frighten each other with stories of an angry**

God that will lay to waste all who do not obey. You get pleasure from thinking of all the horrendous ways your enemies will be made to suffer. You will listen to someone expound for hours about how you are a sinner. They tell you God will only forgive you if you believe and do as they do. Some are so self-righteous they believe that only they are worthy to enter paradise. They carry the lie to their Brothers and Sisters, saying, 'if you believe as we, you will be saved.'"

Waving his arms in the air, he walked about the room, almost yelling. *He must have learned this from some of the evangelists I have seen on television*, I thought.

"When most of you pray, do you ask for guidance? No, all that is asked for are things you want. 'Oh, Heavenly Father, please make *me* worthy, make the world a better place for *me* and *mine*, help *m*e to teach the sinners so as they may be in heaven with *me*.' Or you try to bargain with God. 'If you do this for *me*, I will do that for you.'

"Some try to buy their way into heaven by giving money to their church or the poor. I have seen this when I walked the earth. The killing of animals and the burning of their bodies for sacrifice, or paying someone else to do it for them. Thousands of years have passed since then and still only few have heard. People have always sat and wondered why I rant and rave the way I do.

"It is beyond my realm of knowing why so much time is wasted on all this pettiness. If only you truly knew of God's love. You will learn, I promise, you will learn."

He dropped his hands to his side, bowed his head, turned around, walked through the glass door and was gone. The next time I see the angel, I think I'll ask him who this mad monk is.

Bless your heart

CHAPTER 2
Write It Down for It Is Important

I was still thinking about doing the baptism a month later. During this time there was no angel, no monk, no anything. Donna kept asking if I had seen the angel again, but I hadn't. Then one night Donna set the alarm clock to wake us before sunrise, and placed a bottle of wine and two bowls on the table by the door. "Let's do the baptism in the morning," she said.

I was glad she brought it up.

We don't normally eat breakfast until late morning, but since I needed to fast before doing the baptism, I wanted to eat something. Because I needed to be still until the sun reached its highest point in the sky, I started thinking that I should have done this back in January when the days were shorter and I didn't have to be still for so long. Well, I could see now that all that waiting does is cause more waiting. I put it off for as long as I could because I didn't want to find out what was next. Did I want to? Well, to be honest, I was a little afraid.

My life was going along just fine and I didn't need any angel coming around to mess it up. What if this angel tells me I have to give up my wife, my dogs, my home and everything else I've worked so hard for? How do you tell an angel, if it comes to Donna and the dogs, he will have to find someone else? It has taken me forty eight years to get here and I don't want to give it up.

That's when I began thinking that God would not have given me all this just to take it away. God is going to do with me what God is going to do, whether I like it or not. Besides, if I can learn to like spinach, I can learn to like whatever God has in store for me.

We went out in the back yard to do the baptism. I was glad we had a six foot fence around it because I didn't want the neighbors seeing what was going on. Only a nut would go out in his backyard, pour wine into a bowl and wash his feet and hands with it. The whole thing kept sounding pretty lame to me, but that's just what we did.

When we were done we picked up everything and started into the house. Donna asked me, "What now?" I told her, "I don't know, but I am getting a splitting headache."

Donna told me later she was driving home after work and thinking about the baptism. She was wondering when she was going to be told what to do with her life. It wasn't like a thought or an idea that came to her. She didn't hear words as in a conversation, but she did hear very clearly. **"What makes you think that I am going to <u>tell</u> you?"**

She understood that she would be guided or shown what to do. Donna was very clear about what she heard and what it meant. She doesn't question it now or need more information to be satisfied with it.

I know something has changed in her.

Donna has a Masters of Business Administration degree with a very strong background in statistics. It is very unusual for her to accept the answer she was given and let it go at that. If she makes a plan for us to go on a vacation, she has a contingency plan just in case and a contingency plan for her contingency plan. No stone is left unturned, no "t" is left uncrossed, no "i" is left undotted when she is looking for something.

A few days after doing the baptism, I was sitting in the backyard watching the waterfall in my lily pond when the angel I had first seen in the doorway of my bedroom came to visit again. This time he was not as dramatic as before. I would like to tell you that he came rising out of the water and stood in the middle of the pond, but it didn't happen like that. He was just there. All I could get out of my mouth was, "Who is

this crazy man?" I started to tell him about what
had happened when God's children came to my
door, when he cut me short.

**"It is Isaac and he is one with God. A
very long time ago he was a prophet that
walked the earth. So great in the
understanding of God's love is he, that when
he left the earth as its teacher, God gave him
leave to return. Isaac has visited many people
over the centuries. Several in your time has he
spoken to, but most of them have run to their
ministers, saying that they had seen the devil
and were afraid of him. For the
unenlightened, he is truly a frightening sight to
behold. Joe, I am going to speak plainly so
you will have no misunderstanding. First of
all, if you think every time you open your
mouth all will listen and hear the words, you**

are as crazy as you think you are -- point taken?"

"Point well taken," I said, "but I have a few hundred thousand questions to ask. O.K.?"

Before I could ask, he said, **"I am from the Lord God and my name you could not pronounce if I told you."**

He did tell me. As beautiful as the sound of his name was, I could not get it out of my mouth. He said I could call him whatever I wanted. I chose "Michael" and asked, "What is the name of the one who sent you?"

I knew that was a mistake. One look at his face told me it was a very big mistake.

With all the authority there is put together, he said, **"No one that walks the earth or breathes the air may know God's name for if they did and spoke it once they would not live** long enough to finish. Many claim to, but none actually do, and this is true. If you are asked who you are sent by, you say, 'I AM' has sent me."

Once again, he knew what I was about to ask before it came out of my mouth.

"Hell is a dump outside of Jerusalem where trash was burned and not a place for damned souls. God loves all his children and would not do that to any of them. Jesus, after seeing how poor in spirit man was, said if he could he would cast the unenlightened into it forever. Out of this came the story of 'if you do not follow God's law, you will go to hell.' Fear will make the disobedient flock of a church obey."

What about the devil, I thought.

"Satan is someone Moses made up in the

Book of Genesis **only to explain the power of God. Man, in his great wisdom, found it useful to blame an unseen force rather than take responsibility for the things he did. Man thinks in terms of greater than or lesser than, as though there is a hierarchy, when in fact there is only God as everything."**

"This is all well and fine, I know what you are saying, but just what does this have to do with me? I am not a member of any church, all I do is ask for guidance in God's will for me. Am I to start a new church or religion? Because if I am, I can tell you I am not the man for the job," I said.

"No one is ever the man or woman for the job. They always say that and some will even suggest someone who they think is just perfect for it."

"That's too bad because that was going to be my next move," I said.

"I know," Michael said, **"starting another church will serve no useful purpose and will only confuse people more than they already are. So over the next two years you will be told of God's will for his children and in this time you will choose three women and four men to take this message out into the world. They will know you and you them. Out of the seven, three will be what you call gay."**

"Excuse me! Hold on there just a minute. Let me get this straight, not that I have anything against gay people, I can tell you right now the churches are going to have a field day with this. Just in case you haven't been keeping up on current events, the Church says that being gay is a sin and forbids it. Do you have any idea what

they are going to have to say about this? My
God, Michael, it is going to be hard enough -- I
mean that would be like me telling the churches
to sell all they own and give it to the poor."

**"I knew you were the right man for the
job. You are beginning to know that which I
have not told you yet. Besides, God doesn't
care what they think, why should you? Let
them forbid what they will, let them be
selective with whomever is let into their
houses. God is not limited in his love and will
not deny the kingdom to anyone."**

Great, I thought, *I will probably get
nailed to a cross or burned at the stake -- not as
a Christ to be remembered but as a trouble
maker who will serve as an example of what
happens to such a person.*

"My time is over for now. Think about

what I have said, write it down, for it is
important."

Bless your heart

CHAPTER 3
Go in Peace

It had been a week since my last meeting with the angel and I had spent a lot of time thinking about all of this. I wondered where it would all end, but didn't think it would be a good idea to quit my day job. I called my friend Kathleen to see how she was feeling. She has *Lupus* and from time to time she becomes quite ill. She told me she was going to Mexico for about a week for treatment in a hospital. Usually, she would be gone for three weeks but money was tight now and a week would have to do.

"Kathleen," I said, "I want to tell you something that might help and please don't think I'm nuts or anything."

"O.K.," she said, "as sick as I am I'll try anything." I began to tell her of the night in January and about the baptism. I said she could give it a try and see what happens, but also to take her treatment. I had no idea what effect the baptism would have, if any.

She said that she knew there was a reason for our coming together, and from the moment we met she had felt a connection with me. She believed what I told her and said she would call me when she returned.

After saying good-bye and hanging up, I

must admit I started thinking, *what if she came back from Mexico cured?* Would this mean that the baptism is a cure for disease? What would this do in a world of so much illness?

During the week she was gone, I saw Michael again. This time it was in my truck on the way to work. I remember going up the ramp of the 580 freeway headed in the direction of the bay, when I heard Michael say, **"Put on your seatbelt."** I looked over to the passenger seat and there he was -- but then again no he wasn't. *Just what I need,* I thought, *a comedian along for the ride.*

"I see you have found your first of the seven," he said.

"Yeah, and who might that be?" I said sarcastically.

"Kathleen is going to be just fine...not

cured for she has sums to work. She will be a challenging student. Listen to her, though, for as a woman she can see and know things you could miss."

"Look Michael, I have been thinking about your last visit and there are some things I need to know. Such as, where do women and gays fit in? Doesn't the Bible guide people in the direction of God? Aren't we freed from original sin when we are baptized? Wasn't Jesus sent to die for our sins, because we are all sinners and would go to hell? Most important of all to me is what am I supposed to do?" I asked.

"If you could only see that in your questions lay the answer to why, but like the rest of the world you still think that in the beginning you sinned against God and are being punished for it. I tell you truly, when

God created man and woman in spirit, a choice was given to them. They could stay with God in paradise as spirit or become flesh and live on earth. Those that chose to stay are what you know as angels and the rest of you became flesh. However, I say you all were, and are, perfect, whole and complete in God's eyes. You chose the path you are on with no memory of the time before you chose. A promise was given to all that you would return home, your path would start and end. It would wind through the time you have, mixing with others' paths or going off in another direction. Some last for many years and some are over in the blink of an eye, but whichever one you took, it was for an experience. Some you would like and others you would not, but if you do not choose a direction on the path, the

nature of the journey will be chosen for you
and most often you won't like it.

"You have been taught that a sin is bad
and it hurts God. How arrogant of you to
think you are that powerful. I tell you truly,
the only thing God is, feels or does, is LOVE.
The word sin only means 'I have missed the
mark I was aiming at' or 'I made a mistake.'
No one is sitting in heaven with a tally sheet
marking down all the times you have sinned to
see if you have been good enough to get into
heaven.   Are you beginning to see the
obsession you all have with right, wrong, good
and bad? These are judgments you make and
have nothing to do with you coming home, for
all will return in time. I say to you again, you
are perfect, whole, and complete just the way
you are, so act accordingly.   Treat one

another with honor, dignity and respect, but most of all love each other as God loves you.

"I tell you this, NO, Jesus was not given by God to die for the sins of man. You must see that if that was his purpose, he would have died at birth. In the Bible though, it tells a story that was told over and over and over until it was written down and rewritten and rewritten to the point that why he was sent has been lost. That is part of your job; to bring back the light that man's ink has darkened over the years. I will tell you what Jesus said and what he taught. You will write it down, not as a new Bible, but as the truth to guide God's children so that they may be healthy, joyous and abundant on their journey home.

"The Bible has become more important than those it was written for. Perpetuated by

ignorance, it is said that only those who have
the Holy Spirit in them may read it and
understand it. This is a LIE. Interpreting it is
not understanding, besides, everyone has the
Holy Spirit already in them.   Yet the
unenlightened will tell you that you don't and
are a servant of the devil. Any book that tells
you that only *it* speaks for God, lies. Any book
that tells you that if you don't believe in the
book, the kingdom of heaven is lost to you
forever, lies. Anyone who tells you 'come to
me for I will stand with you before God on
your behalf to save your soul,' lies. For only
you will stand before God for your rewards,
and you will stand alone.

"Jesus said when you pray, to go into a
closet by yourself and be quiet, speak to God
like this: 'Our father which art in heaven,

holy is your name, your kingdom come, your will be done, on earth, as it is in heaven. Give us this day, our daily bread, forgiven are our debts and we forgive our debtors. Let us not be in temptation and deliver us from evil.' Don't gather in crowds and pray great prayers for all to hear. Jesus' reason for coming was to teach that when you speak to God, he hears. No one is needed to speak for you and no one can. When you pray for someone, you are giving a blessing as powerful as any priest can give.

"There is no such thing as original sin in the Bible sense of it. Baptism is a ritual borrowed from an ancient religion to signify washing away the ignorance of the existence of God. In this symbolic ritual what you are doing is saying 'I remember.'

"Women are the foundation of natural wisdom and true power. Jesus knew this and always had women with him throughout his life. Only after *Paul of Tarsus* began preaching did women start to lose the place that Jesus recognized they should have. It was the women that taught of Jesus in the catacombs and the loss of their presence has brought the teachings to the place they are now.

"As long as humankind has walked the earth, there have been people who are gay. Perfect, whole and complete just the way they are. You see the more a religion gets accepted, the more it becomes self-righteous in this good versus evil. When forces from the outside begin to let up, it will start putting pressure on itself from the inside beginning with the smallest number of members who act differently or think differently from the majority. Their actions become no better than those of the ones who persecuted them in the beginning and do it now in the name of God or Jesus or the Bible.

"Sex is a gift from God, for you to give to the one you love as your gift of affection. There is nothing bad or wrong about what gender you give this gift to. It is up to you. However, it is the choice of the receiver to accept it or not. If you go whoring, you must understand you are only wasting time. For no bricks are made.

"You can be sure most religions will be up in arms about this, so let them. When they stand before God and find that he doesn't care, I promise they won't either.

**"My time here is over, we will speak
again. GO IN PEACE."**

I don't remember the drive over, or paying
the toll, but there I was, approaching my exit. I
wonder if all people who have no memory of 45
minutes driving time have an angel riding with
them? I don't think so. After work I got to
thinking about what Michael had told me. *I
guess I should write a book*, I thought, but I am a
carpenter, a handyman by trade, and not an
author. Why is it when God wants something
done, it's always someone without the necessary
skills who are chosen to do it? Let's face it, my
handwriting is unreadable and my spelling is
even worse. So I can see why I was chosen to
do this. Yeah, right.

I can't stop thinking about this right and
wrong or good and bad that Michael keeps

bringing up. All right, let's take a look at it and see if it is true that we are obsessed with it. Is it possible our whole way of thinking is influenced by it? If we pull back far enough to see the whole picture, perhaps it will clear some things up. All around us, in the movies, books and television, we just have to see the good guy triumph over the bad guy. For example, Moses (a good guy), was told by God to go into Egypt and tell Pharaoh (the bad guy) to let the Israelites go. That would be a good thing, and not letting them go is a very bad thing, according to Moses (who was a good guy if you don't take into account that he only murdered a high official who was only doing his job). So the Pharaoh, bad guy that he is, up and throws Moses out of Egypt rather than having him executed. Which, by the way, according to the law, was a good thing to do and letting him go was a bad thing. Are you with me so far? Good. It is bad if you are not. This good thing that Moses wants the Pharaoh to do will mean that Egypt loses a great deal of its labor force, which will put the whole country into an economical nightmare and possible collapse, but that is O.K. because it's a good thing to let everybody go.

The point I am trying to make is that throughout history we, as human beings, have put God into the same pattern that we live by. Given that God is only love, it is then impossible that good, bad or right and wrong could exist in the context of love. A simpler way of saying it is *we keep bringing God down to our level.* Although God is above all this pettiness, I sometimes think this is exactly what the church has been instructing us to do. Maybe that is what Michael is telling us. At least, it sure does seem this way.

Bless your heart

Bless your heart

CHAPTER 4
Be At Peace and Teach Only Love

Kathleen called today to tell me what had happened and all I can say is maybe there is something to this. When she arrived in Mexico she was spent. She was too tired to sleep and no matter what she tried, nothing helped. Kathleen started thinking about what I had told her and decided to take a chance. Feeling she had nothing to lose, she took the bottle of wine she had brought along for just this occasion. Picking up a bowl and a towel she headed for the door. It was warm outside and was already well past noon when she sat on the grass away from everyone else. Surely God would overlook and forgive the fact that the wine had not been set out in the sun's path since before noon. Kathleen had been still on the flight down and from the airport to the hospital wondering if God had a reason for her illness. *I have got to get some sleep*, she thought, as she took out the piece of paper where she had written what I had told her.

Setting the bowl on a corner of the paper, so it wouldn't blow away, she poured the wine into it. Coming from her room bare-footed there was no need to take off her shoes, so she closed her eyes and relaxed. She thought, *Joe would not tell me this if it was not true*, and began to wash with the wine. When she had completed washing she said the words I had given her to say. Then she closed her eyes and listened for counsel. Her body started feeling a numb tingling sensation like when an arm or leg has gone to sleep and it starts to wake up. Kathleen described the feeling like a huge magnet pulling something out of her that should not have been there in the first place. Then the feeling was gone and she heard a voice tell her what to do during the next year. Kathleen opened her eyes, picked everything up and went back to her room.

After putting everything away she lay down and fell asleep. She had no idea how long she slept, but when she awoke she felt great and even the doctors were bewildered by how quickly she had recovered. This was just fine with her because usually it took three weeks of treatment before she felt half this healthy.

It was late in the evening when the angel came again to my lily pond where I was contemplating this message. **"It is not fitting that my Lord God's children should suffer,"** Michael said. **"So great has become their longing to know God and the will of God, that they will listen to whomever holds up the Book and claims to know the secret hidden within. The secret which promises everlasting life in paradise with God. Out of fear, they will believe and obey, unto the point of death, that with the authority of a gnat, their leader has threatened the everlasting fires of hell. The Lord God requires not that you die for him, but that you live to love and give comfort to** each other. For death will come to all, so speed it not.

"'I AM' has instructed me to give you these words. It is written that the sins of the fathers are visited upon the children, but I say from this day forward, the debt is paid. Now I say the rewards of the fathers will be visited on the children for a hundred times a hundred generations. It is written that in my house there are many mansions. I say truly, one is yours, that you build brick by brick, with the blessings you give and the deeds you do. A place is set aside for you in paradise to build your mansion and live with me forever. The time is close when I will give to you a book that teaches you to make the bricks. My son, Jesus, has laid the foundation from the time he walked with you.

"In your book it tells of revelation, a vision of things to come, written with the knowledge of that time. It is so corrupted with mysticism and superstition over the centuries, that no man or woman can know its meaning. When 'I AM' speaks it is cloudless, for what I say is what is, no more, no less.

"There will be a great calling of my children when a large number will return home in the blink of an eye. So will many follow in the time to come, yet not to a last judgment. They come to their reward and will dwell with me in their mansions forever.

"It is said that I am a jealous God and you will put no gods before me. This could not be, for I am all that there is and no one is before me. Yet you build great houses with windows of colored glass and fill them with statues carved from stone. You adorn them in jewels, gold and silver, paintings and tapestries to tell stories of what was sacrificed for you.   This you call a house of God, holy ground and say I dwell within. 'I AM' dwells not in these alone. Look you well into the eyes of one another, from the poorest of the poor to the richest of the rich, both in spirit and possessions you will find me there. Look at the fields of grass or flowers and at the deserts, woodlands, jungles and at the animals, I dwell there also. Look to the sunrise or the sunset, look to the stars at night.   Open your eyes and heart for you will see me in all these things. When you have done this, you will know I have no need for such things. It would be fitting to sell them to feed and clothe the needy and turn these great houses into dwellings for those living in the streets.

"You cry out, 'Oh Lord, we need these temples to teach your word and pray in.' Yet I say to you, teach in the fields in the light as Jesus did and all the prophets before and after him did. You need not the great halls for your prayers. Pray as Jesus has taught you.

"'But Lord,' you ask, 'where might we gather to pray for the souls of others?' I tell you this, gather not to pray for those who are sick in spirit. Go to them and make their body, mind and emotions well and the spirit within will be free to do my work.

"You speak of sacrifice and teach that the spilling of blood made a covenant with me, and has since Adam and Eve along with Abraham. You tell of Cain's offering to me being unpleasing, for it was not blood, so I rejected it. You teach that Jesus' blood was shed so I would open the gates of heaven. I say this only once, all things whose blood runs red, who breathe air, have a soul. I gave life to them for my purpose and it must not be shed.

"When you speak of 'Jesus Saves' you belittle what he has done. For you speak as if he did not fulfill what he was sent to do. You listen yet not a word have you heard. Jesus told you when he said, no one comes to the Father but by the Son. By this he made it known that you are saved.

"Think not that in that salvation it gives you license to do that which pleasures only you, casting aside all else. When you do not honor and bless that which is around you, no bricks do you make and your mansion will be fitting in size for you."

With this, Michael became silent and looked at me as if to see what I had to say.

My head was still spinning from all this, but I said, "You know it has always seemed to me that the Bible, Torah and Koran spoke of a vengeful God, one whose punishment is a swift and terrible thing to behold when he is displeased. Still, he is supposed to be a God of love? That to me is a contradiction in terms. Now I see, if the truth be told, he is all-loving -- period."

"Yes Joe, God is, and with so great a love for you all, that if you could know the feeling of only the smallest portion of God's love, you would weep tears of joy that would fill rivers," Michael stated.

"I hear what's being said about Jesus, but as regarding him making it known that we are saved, why has it been so difficult for us to understand this concept?" I asked.

"Jesus was sitting with his disciples teaching, when Simon said to him, 'Master you tell these truths, yet how is it they fall on so many deaf ears? The people gather to listen and know not of what you speak.' Jesus told him, 'My teachings are not for this age but for the next.' Jesus knew that the spiritual state of most people was such that it would take two thousand years before mortals could rise to a level where they could understand what he is teaching. Take a look around your world. Do you not see many beginning to really know the truths Jesus taught?"

"Yes, I do. I see more and more people looking for the truth. I see people returning to the old established religion, and calling the truth

New Age thinking. Some say New Age thinking
is the work of the devil because it talks about the
signs of the zodiac."

**"You know what I have said about the
devil so speak of it to me no more. One of your
teachers has given you the knowledge of what
an age is. I say truly to you, the age that is
coming is new for it has never been nor will be
again. So you see it is a New Age. The zodiac
is just a heavenly clock that measures the
movement of the earth, planets, sun and stars.
But, since the early religions thought the earth
was the center of the universe and said
everything that moved around the earth was
being pushed by angels, anything else was
blasphemy."**

My teacher, Alexander Everett, explained
it to me this way. An age lasts two thousand

years and it will take about one hundred years as a transition from one age to the next. Each age has specific characteristics. The churches believe this is nonsense. Could be, but let's take a look. The age we are in now is Pisces, which started around the birth of Jesus. Now, Pisces is a water sign of the zodiac; its symbol is that of two fishes. The early Christians used a fish as their sign, and not the cross. A common occupation of the age was a fisherman because fish is the food of the age. Which might be why Jesus said, "Come with me and I will make you fishers of men." When someone was baptized, water was used. Jesus walked on water to signify he had dominion over the age. He changed water into wine to signify the beginning of his teachings from his time to the next age. When Jesus gave The Sermon on the Mount, he fed the people fish and bread, which symbolized the blending of the ages.

If you go back another two thousand years, you are in the age of Aries the ram, which is a fire sign. God appeared to Moses, for example, on top of a fiery mountain in a bush that was on fire. Moses led his people through the wilderness at night following a pillar of fire. A common occupation of that age was herding sheep. The food of the age was ram or sheep. The baptism of the Jewish people was done with fire. Go back another two thousand years and you are in the age of Taurus the bull and it is an earth sign. This age was the time of building. This is when people started to build great cities, pyramids and monuments. The occupation of the age was that of builder, and if you look at the mason's square, you might notice it came out of

Egypt. The food of the age was beef. Have you ever heard the expression, *prepare the fatted calf*?

Now then let's talk about the coming age -- the age of Aquarius. This is an air sign and its symbol is that of a man with a jar of water who is pouring the water out on the earth. What this symbolizes is the pouring of knowledge on the earth. He is also holding stalks of grain. The occupation of the age will be farming and other things related to growing. The food of the age is grains and other things that are grown. As for the pouring of knowledge, take for instance the invention of the light bulb, radio and television and the period of time that it took to invent and develop these. Roughly, in the last one hundred years. In the last part of this century alone, as we make the transition into the new age, we move from light bulbs to lasers, from digital watches and calculators to supercomputers, from the telegraph and telephone to the information superhighway. The inference I'm making is not what we have acquired in our knowledge and technology, but the astounding rate in which we are acquiring it.

You may say, so what does all this have to do with what Jesus taught? Well, according to the Bible, Jesus told Peter and John, "Go and prepare the Passover meal for us." They asked him where he wanted the meal to be. Jesus told them to go into the city and that a man carrying a jug of water would meet them (sound familiar?). "He will show you a large room upstairs, already furnished. Make preparations for us there," Jesus said.

I could understand at least some

similarities in what Jesus said and did and the symbols of the New Age. Doesn't it say in Genesis somewhere that God put the stars in the sky as a sign and to mark the change of seasons?

Then I asked Michael about not eating anything that bleeds red. "Does this mean that animals have souls too?" After asking this, I started thinking. *That would mean dogs, cats, pigs, cows, whales, lions and tigers and bears. Oh my! Good-bye bacon, steak, eggs and fried chicken.*

"Yes, they do," Michael said. **"If their blood is red they have souls, not as advanced as yours but souls nonetheless. You and your kind will use them for food for only a little while and then will no more. In the time to come, food is to be in such abundance, animals will not be needed as food. All this will be told**

to you when the time comes for *The Book of Bricks*."

"Yeah, I want to talk to you about that," I said. "You see, I figured out for myself it has to do with making bricks for our mansions. So I guess it's about all these laws we will be given that tell us if we obey them we get bricks and if we don't, we won't. Right?"

"Are you not listening to the message God is giving? This is not a book of laws that you must obey so you will be given bricks. If you need a comparison, it is as a builder's manual or an instruction book. This book tells you how to make bricks, not what you must do to get them. Too many laws have been made for you to keep or break that have earned little. This book will give you what you need to know, so that many will the bricks be for

your mansions in paradise."

"O.K. I understand the distinction. Now, when do I get the book?"

"When you are ready in God's eyes to receive it. Take heart, Joe, for the time is close at hand."

"Well, I guess if it has taken two thousand years to get this far, sometime in my life is soon enough. As far as I can see, in our talk today, we as God's children have no idea of God's love for us. Yet we want to be with God so much that we will listen to anyone who tells us he knows how to get us there, from fear of going to hell, which doesn't exist anyway. If someone comes along and tells us he is Jesus, we kill ourselves because he says Armageddon is just around the corner. We do what we are told because we don't understand what was written originally in the Bible, the Torah and the Koran. We practice idolatry in our churches through our ignorance. We are borderline cannibals because we eat other creatures that have souls. And all the time we tell ourselves that a vengeful and jealous God had his son killed to open the gates of heaven. Who would send Jesus back a second time to toss most of us into hell anyway? Because he didn't get the job done right the first time, he would have to come back to save us. Does that just about sum it up?"

"What you speak has great truth in the way it has been, yet I say to all of you, Jesus will not return, for he is with you even now. I tell you truly also he is not alone. The Holy Spirit is with him as a sister in what will be done."

"So tell me, how we will know Jesus or

his sister when we see them and what are they supposed to do, and what are they going to teach us?"

"You will know them in this way, he and she will be together *and* they will be apart. They will be young *and* they will be old. Dressed in rags or dressed in fine clothing. They are well *and* they are lame. They are fair *and* they are dark. The way you will know most of all is that they are in need.

"They have not come to teach, but to learn from you. Compassion, kindness and giving is what you will teach them. You will know not who they are, yet they will know you.

"What they will do is open a time for you to make many bricks by the deeds and blessings you shower on them. Be generous in this and an abundant supply of bricks will be

yours. Act meagerly and you will make no bricks.

"My time is over for now, be at peace and teach only love."

With that he was gone, fading away like before, leaving me thinking about what he said. I thought about my Roman Catholic upbringing. In second or third grade during catechism class, we were doing the *who, what and where is God* thing. I did just fine with "God is love" and with "God created heaven and earth and all living things." These things the nun, Sister Mary Elizabeth, explained in no uncertain terms; it was fact, no ifs, ands or buts about it. Where I got into trouble was with the *where* thing. Now this nun, if I even have her name right, was the spitting image of Sister Theresa. I can still see her kind and loving eyes looking through that set of what seemed to be strong yet inexpensive and very unfashionable eyeglasses. She had the sweet and wise face of anyone's best-loved grandmother, hazel eyes with graying eyebrows, a cute little pug nose and thin lips set above a chin so smooth and round, it would have fit perfectly on the nape of your neck if she hugged you. Her face was all I could see because a white band covered her forehead. A white collar ran around her neck, the rest of her was covered in black. She also had on what looked to me at the time to be a white cardboard bib. I guessed it was so she wouldn't spill anything on her black robe when she was eating. At least this made sense to me at the time.

"Where is God?" she asked. And all the children in the class replied, "God is everywhere."

"That's right," she said. "God is in the trees, in the animals, in the ocean, in the rocks, in heaven and on earth. So you see God is everywhere. Except in you. Because you were born with original sin. Until you're baptized in the Church, you will never go to heaven."

Even in second or third grade, with my limited wisdom and intelligence, it occurred to me, *Wait a minute, this stinks. She just said that God is everywhere. And now she says that God is not within us because we are sinners.* I couldn't understand this. So thirsting for knowledge was I, that my hand shot up into the air immediately.

Her kind eyes looked at me and she said, "Yes, Joe, do you have a question?"

"Yes, Sister," I said. "I don't understand how God can be everywhere and not be in me because either God is EVERYWHERE or he's ALMOST everywhere, but he can't be everywhere and not be everywhere at the same time. Could you explain this to me -- because I really don't understand."

Standing at the blackboard behind her desk, something in Sister Mary Elizabeth's eyes had changed as she said, "So, you don't understand." She picked up a book from her desk and walked to the end of the aisle farthest away from me and proceeded to walk the length of it. I figured she was going to come down my aisle from the back. We had always been told to look forward in class because there was nothing in the back we needed to see. I heard her soft steps coming down the aisle from behind me. Sitting there I knew that in a few moments, that which I did not understand would be made clear to me. Her footsteps stopped. I heard a THUD, as the crashing blow of the book reached the back of my head, sending me sprawling in the aisle. I tried to pick myself up off the floor, as my senses began to come back to me. I looked up and saw what used to be a sweet grandmother type. She had transformed into a vicious attack dog, "Now do you understand? Now do you understand?" she growled.

Humbled by my stupidity for asking a question that would get this kind of response, in a low voice I replied, "Yes Sister, I understand." "That's good," she said, "because the Church wants everyone to go to heaven. And it really doesn't make any difference whether you understand or not. You just have to believe what the Church tells you."

As she walked back to her desk, the other

children looked at me as though I were an idiot and my embarrassment was almost overwhelming. I did understand. I was absolutely sure I understood. I understood that I would never not understand again.

The reason for telling you this story is to give you the background of my religious upbringing. I also want you to understand a conflict that is going on in me. I would have liked to live a saintly life in accordance with the Scriptures, but I haven't. All the things I learned as a child about God stayed in the back of my head and still haunts me today. I think I know what must have been going on in the minds of the people Jesus had been teaching. If you are brought up to believe a certain way and all your life you do the best you can to live up to these teachings, when someone tells you it is all different, then you have a choice of at least two belief systems. That is a luxury I no longer have. I don't know what someone else would do, I only know what I must do. I do trust that God knows where this is all going.

Bless your heart

CHAPTER 5
Begin

I looked up from where I sat and saw Michael. "Oh, hi Michael, I started writing down what you have been telling me, but you probably already know that," I said.

"I do. Blessed are the works you have chosen to do. Blessed are you, for you hear God's words and you follow, setting aside that which you think you know. The path you have

**taken may not be as difficult to walk as you
think, for 'I AM' walks with you."**

"That is wonderful to know, but at this
point I feel as though I am walking this path in
the dark," I said and saw him smile.

"Joe," he said. **"You walk not in
darkness, but in light. When you emerge from
a place that is dim into the bright sunlight, it
will take time before you see clearly. In that
time you want to cover your eyes for such a
light brings discomfort. Soon you will be
accustomed to it and see wonders that were
only shadows in the darkness before."**

(I wish I had a pair of sunglasses for this,
I thought to myself).

**"For the first wonder, you will call upon
the land of the bear and say to them, "'I AM'
has sent me that you may be strong among**

nations. Take your boat that sails under the sea, and go you to the valley of the star. In the deepest part of this valley you will thrust a hollow rod seven feet into the bottom. Take what you have gathered there back to your land, give it to your men of wisdom and healing. In this lies the cure for two great plagues that are in all lands. Before a year is finished you will find it. You may ask a fair price for your labor and medicine. In return you will give one seventh to my servant that has brought you this. If you do these things great riches will be yours.'"

I asked, "I think I know what country you are talking about, but why not my own? Also what is this one seventh given to me for, is it like tithing?"

He answered simply. **"Your country**

would question it for too long and many would die needlessly. Look to the birds of the field. Neither do they sow nor reap, yet their heavenly father feeds them. No, it is not tithing. Tithing was established by the churches as a tax to support itself and the poor. Over the years the church forgot the poor and became rich, powerful and greedy. Giving little to the poor, they thought the tithing belonged to them and still do today. It is to be that only one seventh may be given to those who teach God's words. Of that one seventh, a full five will be given to the poor and only two may be kept to live on.

"The gift of one seventh is so that your brothers and sisters need not suffer. A gift is something that is given and not owed. Say to them that rob from God's children with their tithing that they make no bricks today.

"Say this also to those who have become wealthy on the tithing, whether they display it as gold encrusted with jewels in great houses or hide it in vaults or sell the jewels or melt down the gold into the coin of the realm. Take once, and once only, one fourth of your riches gathered by tithing and keep it to live on. Take the remaining three fourths and heal the sick, feed the hungry, clothe the naked and house the homeless. If you choose not to do this, all will be taken. You will not be left with even the fourth and no bricks do you make."

"Well, as long as we are on a roll here, is there any more good news you would like me to break to the Christian community while I'm at it?" I asked.

"Tell those who lay hands on their

flock, healing sickness and twisted bodies, to stop acting as if they had anything to do with it. Only faith can do this. 'Physician, heal thyself' means just that. You and your faith are all you need to heal yourself. Jesus told you that, so believe.

"Go to Kathleen and say to her, 'Get your house in order for you are called to do God's work.' It was a woman who first saw that Jesus had risen and spoke to him. It was the women who told the men of his resurrection. In the time to come, it is women who will see the light first and teach of God's love. It was women who led the men to the light and will do so again. As Mary gave birth to Jesus, so will women give birth to the light that has been in the womb for almost two thousand years. Peter's faith was the rock then, and a woman's wisdom and love for life will be God's rock this time."

"Ah yes, I can see it all now. A world ruled by women, this is going to make some men very happy," I said sarcastically. "So why didn't you just tell a woman all this? Maybe one with typing skills who is not dyslexic, like me?" I added.

"RULE? Women are chosen to nurture and guide. It is in their very nature these things. It is in man's nature to lead. It is only God that will rule out of love for you and your well-being.

"Let me tell you about the birds and the bees."

"Oh very funny, Michael. It is nice to know you have a sense of humor." I said.

"Life starts with a seed that is planted

by the male in the female, grows and then is born. This is how it is with you. That which you are writing is the seed you will give. Like Jesus' earthly father did for him, you will do with these teachings. You will take them out into the world and help them grow. When they are strong enough to stand on their own, you will step aside. Don't worry, I will tell you when that time has come.

"The four men that you will choose represent the four-fold nature of God's children. These four are --

PHYSICAL: to take the teachings out into the world.

MENTAL: to think only of the well being of others.

EMOTIONAL: to love as you are loved by God.

SPIRITUAL: to have a personal relationship with God.

"These four are the signs of balance. As the day is balanced by morning, afternoon, evening and night, the seasons of the year or the points of the compass, all these are in balance with one another.

"The three women stand for the Love God is, the Life is the work God has done and the Light is the result of the union of the other two. This is not new to you, for Alexander teaches this."

"Michael," I responded, "you know this is really going to anger our Holy Mother the Church. There is no way the Church will buy the idea that women could be on the same level or equal to men. To say this is true will undermine the Church's authority. Oh, let's not forget the

Muslims, along with most of the other religions of the world, who will not buy women's equality either.

"You say, 'Being gay isn't a mortal sin and an abomination to God.' 'Women are equal with men.' 'Give back the money that religions have more or less stolen from their members under false pretense.' That last one is going to be the hardest of all for the organized religions to swallow. Now, to top the whole thing off, we are going to tell them they can't rationally use the scriptures as a basis for their authority, because the scriptures are, at the least, disingenuous. That will start one hell of a Jihad."

"The church is neither holy, nor a mother. The people that run it are not being asked to buy anything. I tell you truly, any religion that says it is of God, is actually a

servant of GOD'S CHILDREN, and not the other way around, as it thinks itself to be. Religion has become as unreliable as the servants who steal from their masters. With their ill gotten gains they act as though they are now masters. 'I AM' will dismiss them as servants, if they do not return that which they have stolen and obey those they serve.

"'I AM' has not given them the authority, nor has Jesus or any heavenly host. Just because they have written it in their scriptures does not mean it is so. There is only one authority and it is with God.

"You speak of Jihad, a HOLY WAR -- I tell you this truly -- there is nothing holy about war. War is the violent act to steal or to take back that which was stolen. It was not God that ordered war. It was man who did this. To justify it, he lied, saying 'it was God's will.' Not until the Crusades was war allowed by the Christian church. The head of the Christian church in Rome made war holy, not GOD. Most religions today still think war can be holy if their leaders say it is. The children of Israel and Islam fight with one another and lie when they say it is God's will. Yet they are of the same family of Abraham and the same God he served. When brothers are killing brothers, no bricks are made.

"There will be no Jihad, for God's children will say, 'I give my life to God, who is all loving, and asks only that I live to bring joy and happiness to all. I will not serve any religion in war or die for it.'

"So that you may see that there is no need to fear this Armageddon, 'I AM' has given me the words to tell you of what is truly said in the *Book of Revelation*. You must not speak this knowledge to anyone until you first give it to your seven chosen people. Do you understand?"

I nodded that I did. From the very first words he spoke, I felt that the truth flowed from his mouth.   The sound of his voice was a beautiful melody that carried rich vowels and consonants that warmed my imagination and quieted the panic of my beating heart, giving me the same feeling I had when he told me his name. When he had finished speaking, I didn't even notice. Nor did I notice when he said, **"My time is over for now. Go in peace and teach only love."**

I was in a state of total amazement. What he had told me made complete sense. I felt like

Bones, who, in a classic episode of StarTrek, had been given a mega dose of medical knowledge. What was impossible to understand only moments ago, was now so simple that a child could understand it.

How is it that a message as simple and clear as this could be so misunderstood? No wonder Jesus wept when he saw what man had done to God's words, and so did I. There is something else I did when my tears stopped. I started to laugh, just a little chuckle at first, but the more I thought of the Apocalypse, with its demonic armies in a final battle and Jesus coming out of the clouds like the U.S. cavalry to save the day, the funnier it got until I was almost in hysterics. This was one of those times when tears roll down your cheeks and you can't stop laughing. Well, I roared to myself, I guess you get what you deserve (poetic justice at its finest). Oh, I can see it all now, the religious leaders standing before God and explaining just what possessed them to teach such foolishness like this. I know that the best they'll be able to come up with is, "the devil made me do it."

I had been giving some thought as to how best explain this in the land of the bear. Can't you just see me now, calling the Russian embassy? "I would like to speak to someone about a message I am supposed to give you from God," I would say. But I concluded that what I need to do is just that. Michael didn't say anything to me about making them believe it. He just told me to tell them.

I called Debbie and asked her about how I might get in touch with someone in Russia. She asked if I remembered the two men that were visiting from Russia last summer. I told her I did. She went on to say that maybe I should call or write them. At least they may know how to get it to the right person. She said she would have someone call and let me know their address.

It had been about a week since I had heard from Michael. Every time he told me to do something and I took time to do it, I didn't see him again until I at least started on it. Maybe that is the way it works. He will give me something to do and when I do it, he gives me something else.

Another week had passed before Michael came again. I was sitting at the computer playing a game, and doing quite well, when he said, **"It is time for you to write *The Book of Bricks*."**

"O.K. Michael," I replied, "but first I want to ask you a few things. You see I have been telling some friends of mine of these experiences and they ask me if I know the answers to the important questions now. I told them I had an opinion on almost everything, but answers, no. I would, however, ask you and tell them what you said."

"Ask what you will."

"I have a list of things to ask," I began. "First of all, why has God made evil if he is all loving?"

"God has not made evil. Your kind has brought it into being. Mankind has become lazy and will not work. It is the easy way to take from others that which you do not have. If you think about it, you will see the truth in what I say."

"What about abortion and the right to life? Should abortion be stopped regardless of what the means are to stop it?" I pursued.

"Your kind is always talking of rights, as if God gave any one group the authority to take life. What you seek is permission to kill in order to stop killing, and you have no such permission. This is not protecting the unborn. This is insanity. I tell you truly, abortion is between a woman and God. God and God alone will give the woman counsel, and interfere you will not."

"What is the true religion of God? I know this sounds like I am asking what religion God belongs to, but I hope you understand my real question. Is he maybe an agnostic that doesn't believe in himself because he just is God?"

"All religions are from God and none are of God. Religion has taken that which God has given and made of it what they understand

it to be. God gave the word and mankind heard what they wanted. To answer your question, all of them and none of them."

"O.K. Now what?"

"**I will be with you as you write and whisper in your soul the words you write. Begin.**"

A note to the reader

The Book of Bricks (contained in chapters
6, 7, 8 & 9) are the exact words of the angel Michael
as dictated to the author.

There has been absolutely no editing done, by either
the author or the publisher.

These are the words of Michael.

CHAPTER 6
The Book of Bricks

You have all chosen to be flesh and blood, with a time to work out sums. You may have as many lifetimes as you need. Yet there is a point when all must be done. This time is known as the Grand Gathering when God's children will be called home. A quickening has begun at this time before the gathering, so you may add bricks to your mansion. So long have you been away from your home, that you have forgotten it. You have built a new home out of dust in a far away land. This house you will not keep, for it is of worldly things. Many of you have labored for worldly things for long in years, while setting aside your real reason for coming to earth.

I give this book so you may remember and build your mansions in paradise. This is not a book of laws that you must obey. Nor is it a book that you may judge your neighbor by. There is no punishment if you do not use it to make bricks. You are given this book out of love, so that you may make the number of bricks you want. Your time is short before the calling, and when you are called your mansion will be complete. Not one brick will be added or taken away from your labors. That which you have built will be yours for all time. When your mansion is finished you will come home to it. God will furnish it with all the wondrous things your imagination can hold. You will share paradise with all you have ever loved or were loved by. I tell you now. You must never set this book above one another. You will not hold it as holy or sacred. You will worship it not. It will not be kissed or held with affection in any way.

The Book of Bricks is written in three parts. Each is equal unto the other and none is greater or lesser in value. The first text is of Blessings. This book deals with the emotional training. The second is the text of Giving. This book trains the mind. The third text is of Deeds. This book is to train the body. The three stand as separate legs of a tripod. Each leg is planted firmly on a solid spot. They rise upwards toward a center that holds the platform. On the platform is mounted a transom (the soul), to make sure your direction is straight and level.

CHAPTER 7
The Book of Blessings

That this leg may stand on solid ground
and your blessings begin, once-blessed are you
who take this leg to heart. Some will find it the
easiest to set, while others find it almost
impossible. Yet set it firmly you will by giving
your first blessing to you. Bless my soul for I
am a child of God. Bless my heart for it beats

to serve you my God and your children. God has made me perfect, whole and complete for I am in God's own image and likeness. With this knowledge I am all I need to be. I set this leg as the foundation of God's will for me and all others.

The deep feeling of infinite compassion is not just an emotion. This oneness with God sets in motion an uncontrollable desire. Your soul wishes only love and well-being for a person, place or thing. When this happens you make a brick by saying "Bless its heart." There is no blessing so small that it does not make a brick. Saying this only so a brick will be added to your mansion is done in vain, for no brick is made.

Should you see a child crying for whatever

reason. Know they are in pain and bless their heart. A BRICK IS MADE.

See you tears in the eyes of a man or woman. Know they are in pain or joy and bless their heart. A BRICK IS MADE.

See you someone who is in anger or rage. Know they are in pain for some reason and bless their heart. A BRICK IS MADE.

See you someone who is blind. They see not the wonders you do and bless their heart. A BRICK IS MADE.

See you someone who is deaf. They hear not the music of nature and bless their heart. A BRICK IS MADE.

See you someone who cannot speak. Their voice sings not the language you share and bless their heart. A BRICK IS MADE.

See you someone who is lame. They shuffle

with difficulty in the dance of life and bless their heart. A BRICK IS MADE.

See you someone who is disfigured. They are ugly only in the eyes that hold them so and bless their heart. A BRICK IS MADE.

See you someone who is poor. They know not of the abundance that is theirs and bless their heart. A BRICK IS MADE.

See you someone who is hungry. They have forgotten how to feed themselves and bless their heart. A BRICK IS MADE.

See you someone who is naked or in rags. They know not how to clothe themselves and bless their heart. A BRICK IS MADE.

See you someone who is homeless. They have forgotten how to shelter themselves and bless their heart. A BRICK IS MADE.

See you someone who is a drunkard or an

addict. What they take to numb their pain is now its cause and bless their heart. A BRICK IS MADE.

See you someone who is slow of wit. Their mind is in a cloud of darkness struggling to be free and bless their heart. A BRICK IS MADE.

See you someone who is a criminal. They have lost their faith and bless their heart. A BRICK IS MADE.

See you someone who steals a childhood. They have had their childhood stolen and bless their heart. A BRICK IS MADE.

See you someone who takes a place before you. They take from you only that which has been taken from them and bless their heart. A BRICK IS MADE.

See you someone who respects you not.

They have no respect for themselves and bless their heart. A BRICK IS MADE.

See you someone who has taken a life. They know not what they have truly done and bless their heart. A BRICK IS MADE.

See you someone who is with disease. They know not that they could be well and bless their heart. A BRICK IS MADE.

See you someone who belittles others. They see themselves as unimportant and bless their heart. A BRICK IS MADE.

See you someone who robs others. They only rob bricks from themselves and bless their heart. A BRICK IS MADE.

See you someone who cheats others. They only cheat themselves out of bricks and bless their heart. A BRICK IS MADE.

See you someone who hollers at others.

They want to be heard but know not how and bless their heart. A BRICK IS MADE.

See you someone who lays a hand to others. They only strike bricks from their walls and bless their heart. A BRICK IS MADE.

See you a sick or injured animal. Bless its heart. A BRICK IS MADE.

See you any animal that has died. Bless its heart. A BRICK IS MADE.

See you the meat on your table. Know you that the animal gave up its life that you may be fed. Ask forgiveness and bless its heart. A BRICK IS MADE.

Let not a day go by that you have not given blessings. Open your heart to the world around you. Find in all things a reason to give blessings.

Your God has blessed you and all else.

God's blessings come as easily as the rising and setting of the sun. Should not yours be given with the love you hold in your heart? Should you not bless all things around you that have been given to you? Think not that it makes no difference and it is but a small and unimportant thing to do. For I tell you truly, there is no blessing that you can give that is insignificant. Any blessing you give is a brick and will be given by God back to you unto the "nth" degree.

CHAPTER 8
The Book Of Giving

That this leg may stand on solid ground and your giving begin, twice blessed are you who take this second leg to heart. That you may give to others, you must give to yourself. Forgive yourself all that keeps you from greatness. I am a child of God and from my soul I give. My heart beats to give to you, my God, and your children. I give myself the knowledge that I am made in God's image and likeness to be perfect, whole and complete. I am all I need to be to set the second leg as the foundation of God's will for me and all others.

The gift of giving is more than the mental process of I think I should, therefore I give. Be responsible in giving. If others benefit from your gift and you or your family is left wanting, this is not responsible giving, this is suffering. Be you abundant so others may prosper also. God has not meant for you to go hungry so others may eat. You are not to go naked so others may be clothed. You shall not live in the streets, that others may live in a mansion. There is no gift so small that it does not make a brick. But to give only that a brick is added to your mansion is done in vain, for no brick is made.

Be you loving to yourself as God loves you. A BRICK IS MADE. Give in return this love to all else around you. A BRICK IS MADE.

Be you kind to yourself that you may know kindness. A BRICK IS MADE. Give this kindness to all else around you. A BRICK IS MADE.

Be you your life's work for it is the cornerstone of life. A BRICK IS MADE. In return see that others have a life's work to be done. A BRICK IS MADE.

Be there food on your table that you will not go hungry. A BRICK IS MADE. Eat no more than you need to live so there will be food for others. A BRICK IS MADE.

Be you clothed so that you will be protected from the heat or cold. A BRICK IS MADE. Give that which you do not use to those in rags. A BRICK IS MADE.

Be you sheltered that you will be dry and warm. A BRICK IS MADE. Make it that all have shelter. A BRICK IS MADE.

Be you receiving when someone gives to you. A BRICK IS MADE. That others may receive from what you give. A BRICK IS MADE.

Be you filled in your basic requirements and that of your family. A BRICK IS MADE. See you then that others have the same. A BRICK IS MADE.

Be you relieved from your pain. A BRICK IS MADE. Give relief to those in pain.   A BRICK IS MADE.

Be you sightful though you are blind. A BRICK IS MADE. Give you eyes to those who cannot see. A BRICK IS MADE.

Be you listening though you cannot hear. A BRICK IS MADE. Give you ears to those who cannot hear. A BRICK IS MADE.

Be you heard though you cannot speak. A BRICK IS MADE. Hear you those that cannot speak. A BRICK IS MADE.

Be you active though you are lame. A BRICK IS MADE. Put those who cannot move into motion. A BRICK IS MADE.

Be you beautiful though you appear disfigured. A BRICK IS MADE. See you beauty in those who seem to be ugly. A BRICK IS MADE

Be you healthy though you are ill. A BRICK IS MADE. Give health to those who are sick. A BRICK IS MADE.

Be you seduced not to use drug or drink in ways for which it was not intended. A BRICK

IS MADE. Give freedom to the enslavement of these, to those who are in its bondage. A BRICK IS MADE.

Be you quick in mind though you are slow. A BRICK IS MADE. Take time to understand those whose wit is dim. A BRICK IS MADE.

Be you honest though you have committed crimes. A BRICK IS MADE. Hold responsible ones who have committed a crime and then forgive them. A BRICK IS MADE.

Be you caring of a child's well-being though yours may have been taken. A BRICK IS MADE. See that others are caring of children and their well-being. A BRICK IS MADE.

Be you courteous to all and assume no place that is not yours. A BRICK IS MADE. Allow the elderly, lame and children to go before you. A BRICK IS MADE.

Be you respectful though you may have been disrespected. A BRICK IS MADE. See that others respect one another. A BRICK IS MADE.

Be you one who does not take a life. A BRICK IS MADE. Give mercy to and yet hold responsible one who has taken a life. A BRICK IS MADE.

Be you knowing that you are of greatness, though you may have been belittled. A BRICK IS MADE. Give in return greatness to those who have been belittled. A BRICK IS MADE.

Be you trustworthy taking not that which you have not been given or have not earned. A BRICK IS MADE. Give trust to others that they may be trustworthy. A BRICK IS MADE.

Be you soft-spoken with respect in your

voice, though you may have been hollered on. A BRICK IS MADE. Require others to softly and with respect speak to each other. A BRICK IS MADE.

Be you gentle with your touch though you have been made to smart by a heavy hand. A BRICK IS MADE. See you that no one is laid a hand to. A BRICK IS MADE.

Be you so loving of an animal that you make room in your home for it. A BRICK IS MADE. Give you sanctuary to the animals in need. A BRICK IS MADE.

Be you caring of the animals making them neither sick nor injured. A BRICK IS MADE. Give you health to those animals in need of it. A BRICK IS MADE.

Be you fed by that which has not red blood. A BRICK IS MADE. Spare the life of an animal that you would otherwise use for food. A BRICK IS MADE.

Be you respectful of all life. A BRICK IS MADE. Take not so much that there is no more to come. A BRICK IS MADE.

Let not a day go by that you have not been giving. Open your mind to the world around you. Find in all life a reason and something to give. God gives life every second of every day. Should not you render with the same thoughts a life to be spared? Should you not think that all life is as precious as your own?

Think you not that it makes no difference or that any gift you give is insignificant. For I tell you truly, there is no gift that you give too little that it will not be given back to you to the "nth" degree.

Bless your heart

CHAPTER 9

The Book of Deeds

That this leg may stand on solid ground
and your deeds begin, thrice blessed are you
who take this third leg to heart. You have
blessed and you've given. Take that which
needs to be done and do it yourself. Say: "I
am a child of God. My heart beats to do God's
will for his children and me. This I can do, for

God has made me perfect, whole and complete. I am made in God's own image and likeness. Therefore I am all I need to be and the works I do now anchor fast this leg."

The work that is done in your name is blessed. The work that is done by your name and moneys is twice blessed. The work that is done by your hand is thrice blessed. When you see a need to be filled, you first feel it in your heart. Then you are moved emotionally with the desire to have it not be so. Your mind will search for a way to have it otherwise. Then you take to task this need and with your hands you fill this need. There is no deed so small that it does not make a brick. Woe unto you who do this only so that a brick is added to your mansion. This is done in vain, for no brick is made.

I, by my hand, end the pain of a child. THREE BRICKS ARE MADE.

I, by my hand, dry the eyes of a man or woman. THREE BRICKS ARE MADE.

I, by my hand, soothe the anger and rage. THREE BRICKS ARE MADE.

I, by my hand, lead the blind through the darkness. THREE BRICKS ARE MADE.

I, by my hand, speak the music of the deaf that they might hear. THREE BRICKS ARE MADE.

I, by my hand, hear the voice of the speechless that they may sing. THREE BRICKS ARE MADE.

I, by my hand, bind up the lame that they may travel their path and dance through life. THREE BRICKS ARE MADE.

I, by my hand, give comfort to the ill that they may have health. **THREE BRICKS ARE MADE.**

I, by my hand, open the eyes of all to see the beauty, that none will shun away from the disfigured. **THREE BRICKS ARE MADE.**

I, by my hand, raise up the poor that they may make their own way and have an abundant life. **THREE BRICKS ARE MADE.**

I, by my hand, feed the hungry so they will learn to feed themselves. **THREE BRICKS ARE MADE.**

I, by my hand, dress the naked and those in rags with clean clothes, that they will clothe themselves. **THREE BRICKS ARE MADE.**

I, by my hand, build shelter with the homeless, that they will build shelter for themselves. **THREE BRICKS ARE MADE.**

I, by my hand, bring the tactility of love to replace the numbness in the drunkard or the addict, that they might feel the joy of life and release their pain. THREE BRICKS ARE MADE.

I, by my hand, remove the clouds of darkness, so the dim of wit will see they too have a place of importance. THREE BRICKS ARE MADE.

I, by my hand, hold those who commit a crime responsible to repay that which was taken, and they are forgiven that which is paid. THREE BRICKS ARE MADE.

I, by my hand, will make straight that which I have made crooked through mistake or knowledge, for I am honest. THREE BRICKS ARE MADE.

I, by my hand, give care and see to the

well-being of a child, that they may pass through childhood unmolested by word or action. THREE   BRICKS ARE MADE.

I, by my hand, will make way for those who need a passage, be they young or old. THREE BRICKS ARE MADE.

I, by my hand, will not allow a life to be taken nor will I allow a life to be prolonged to suit my purpose. THREE BRICKS ARE MADE.

I, by my hand, will hold up to greatness those who have been belittled.   THREE BRICKS ARE MADE.

I, by my hand, will not take the life of an animal nor will I prolong it to suit my purpose. THREE BRICKS ARE MADE.

I, by my hand, will open my house and heart to an animal. I will care for its needs and love it as if it were my child. THREE BRICKS ARE MADE.

I, by my hand, will only build that which does not destroy the sanctuary of animals in the wild. THREE BRICKS ARE MADE.

I, by my hand, will set my table with food that does not run red with blood. THREE BRICKS ARE MADE.

Let not a day pass that a deed has not been done. Open your arms to the world around you. Find in all things a deed that you might do. God does for you more than you will ever know. Should you not do the same? Should not your deeds be given as freely?

Think you not that what you do makes little difference, or that it is an insignificant act. For I tell you truly no deed is so small that it will not be returned to you unto the "nth" degree.

Carry this book with you. When you know not what to do, it will guide you. As a builder's manual gives you the measurements of work to be done on the straight and level, so does this book give you measurements to live your life, that it may be straight and level. Go you now into the world and teach only love for God is with you all.

I didn't see Michael leave nor was I aware of his leaving. Somehow I knew he was with me because on two parts of the book I got stuck and twice he helped me out. The first was when I was writing *The Book of Giving*. I kept starting with, "Give you" this or that and then could not go any further with it. That's when I said, "O.K. Michael, you have got to help me on this one. I can't get past 'Give you.'" **"It is not that you give these, but you are these things to give,"** came booming in my ear.

The second time I got stuck, I was sitting at the computer writing *The Book of Deeds*. "Do you" this I would write or "Do you" that, and it looked and it sounded like it didn't make any sense. So again I asked Michael to give me a hand. I wrote it over and over with the same results but it still came out the same. How the hell am I to start this book about deeds without someone doing something? *Screw it*, I thought. I am going to the bathroom and then take a nap. No great insight came to me while I was in the bathroom as insights often do. So it was off to bed for me. I went down the hall and back into the spare bedroom we use for an office to hit *SAVE* and then turn off the computer.

"Whoa," I said to myself as I saw the screen. "Of course, what else could it be?" The words read **"I by my hand"**. After seeing what Michael must have typed, I just sat down and wrote until *The Book of Bricks* was finished.

I went back and read what Michael had me write. I know that I wrote it down as if it came from me, but I have no memory of writing it or thinking it up. As I read, I could see how it could work. This is not a list of shalls and shall nots. These are not things that, if disobeyed, are a sin to be punished for. These are simple things we can do. We can incorporate them into our everyday lives without a lot of muss or fuss. Everything in the books is giving us the freedom to be who we are and there is nothing that condemns us for what we are or what we have done. I like this just fine but it appears to take all control away from religions. It is just like getting an instruction book on how to make our lives work. As with any instruction book, we can choose to use it or not. The really great thing is, that what we are building is not worthless, even if we have a few parts left over. It's not like anyone has ever put anything together with parts left over. Remind you of anyone you know?

I am thrilled to think that I can give a blessing to someone or something as a child of God. This opens a whole new existence that I had no idea of, in which I get to play an important part. The best thing of all, is that everyone else does too. Maybe this is what Jesus, Mohammed, Buddha and all the others tried to tell us. Wouldn't it be awesome if we heard it this time? What if everyone in the world really understood this?

What kind of a life and world could we have?

Imagine what it would be like to have a relationship with God that is not of judgment and punishment, but a relationship of love that gives you direction home, rather than hoops that you must jump through to get there. Do you really think God would make it hard to get home? I don't. I think the directions were lost or forgotten years ago. I don't think any religion would purposely misplace directions as easy to follow as these are. Even if religious leaders thought uneducated people could not understand what the directions were saying, what possible motive could they have for keeping it from the people? Well, it is just beyond me, unless the churches just misinterpreted and let it go at that. It is going to take awhile for me to incorporate this into all aspects of my life, because I don't think I have arrived yet. I do believe it to be an ongoing process that will allow me to grow in my relationship with God. Given the magnitude of what is written in *The Book of Bricks*, I just may have to learn to walk, before I can run home, though my path there is clearer than it has ever been. The journey may be a little easier knowing that no one is watching me, to make sure I'm doing it right. I don't have to worry about getting there on time, because I will get there when I get there. Isn't it nice to know we have been sent out to play and grow on this big adventure we are all on, until it is time to come home?

Bless your heart

CHAPTER 10
Good-bye

It's the next day. I just got back from giving an envelope to Deb to send to our friend in Russia. In it was what I had written so far along with a letter. I asked in the letter if he could give it to somebody who might do something with it. If not, could he tell me whom I might send it to. Well, I'll just see what happens and take it from there.

I went to see Deb again to give her what I had written since the last time I had seen her. She read it and we talked about it the next time we met. Today she said a few things that got me to wondering. She told me her husband thought the land of the bear might be California. "Yeah, it could very well be," I told her, "but I got the impression it was a country and not a state. I could be wrong in thinking it was a country and if nothing comes of it, I'll know I was, in fact, wrong about it." She asked me something else. How am I doing with all of this and what if people don't believe what I have written? I told her, "Hey look, it is not my job to make people believe. All that I'm supposed to do so far is to write it down and get it out for people to read." Didn't I worry about what my family and friends thought? "People are going to think what they think and I am not going to stop doing what I have been told to do. If an angel tells someone to do something, I think it would be wise to follow directions," I replied.

The next time I see Michael, Deb wants me to ask him about what she is supposed to do. I knew she had not done the baptism yet, so I told her "just do it." Maybe if she did, she might just be told what to do.

"I am not sure that I'm ready for that," she said. "What if I find out, then what? It's no accident you are sharing this with me." she added.

"I know." I said. "There has got to be a reason for sharing it with you, so why don't you just do the baptism and we can both find out. I have to be going now. We'll talk again soon."

I know this is a little scary for Deb. I guess this one is going to take a leap of faith on her part. God knows that's what it took on mine. You know, whenever something comes along that's new or different, it seems people are reluctant to go along with it. Not like this is bad or anything, but imagine where people could be if we were open to new things?

I know something is changing in me since this all started. I find I don't get crazy anymore when I am driving my car. It is not that people have stopped doing dumb things, it's now instead of cussing and yelling, I just say "bless their heart" and let it go at that. It used to be if someone cut in front of me on the freeway, I would speed up and pass them so that they wouldn't think they could put anything over on me, now it's "bless their heart." I chalk it up to they need to be somewhere and can't be late. I don't even push the yellow light any more like I used to. Well, not as much anyway.

I hold open doors for the elderly, women and children. I even let people behind me in line go first. When I hear about someone who has been harmed, I say "bless their heart," and I also bless the heart of the one who did the harming. It is as if I know that something must have happened to them that would cause them to harm someone or something else.

"Joe, you are in doubt. The weight of what you do is heavy with you and you know not how to lessen it."

"No kidding, Michael," I replied. "I thought I would do what I am told to do. In return you would see that things go my way. I bust my hump to get work and make a living, but right now things are slow. It's not like I am asking for the winning lottery numbers or anything like that. Quite frankly, I could use the money."

"Another thing, what about the seven I am to meet? Just when might this happen? All I've got is one and she is working the sums out that she needs to. No one else is in sight and I spend my time writing this book. Well, maybe there is one other person but if it's one of the seven how will I know? Do I just go up to people and ask them to follow me? Tell them I will make them fishers of men, like Jesus did or what? Sorry about complaining, but do you think you could give me a hand here?"

"What would you have me do? Give you all the work you could handle, give you the lottery numbers you ask for? Why do you ask for these things? Are you poor? Are you

hungry? Are you naked? Are you homeless?
How much have you been blessed since you
said, 'O.K. God, do with me what you will.'?"

He's talking about the time I didn't have a
job, was broke and living in a tree in Big Sur, ("I
can see that things have changed since then," I
said to myself).

"What you have now will look to you as
what you did have then. God knows what you
need and will see that you have it. I promise
money will not be a problem for you and
yours. Worry not that your earthly work is
slow. For you need it not. Soon this book will
be done and you will be about doing God's
work on earth. A hundred times your worth
will you and yours be. In spirit and in riches
will you prosper all the days of your lives.
Trust the path you are on.

"You have seen two more of the seven and they know you. Tell them not to follow you or that you will make them fishers of men, for that time is past. Tell them who would hear, follow that which you teach and this will make of them tillers of souls. I tell you truly, as the farmer tills the soil to open it so that a crop will grow, so shall you and yours open the minds of humanity. Love will grow in the depths of their hearts like a seedling grows into a tree. The crop that has been planted will be raised up to God's light and be gathered in his arms to paradise.

"You are forgiven your complaining for it comes easily to your kind. Did not Jesus ask that the bitter cup pass from him? Did not Abraham, Moses and the prophets complain? You see only the beginning of God's plan and it is almost overwhelming. Therefore you do not know the all of it and because of this you complain.

"Go now and ask those around you what they want you to ask me. I will answer that which they need to know.

"My time is done. Be at peace and teach only love."

Michael was gone just like before. Only a strange thought hit me this time. What if he was really gone? What if he is not coming back? Boy, wouldn't I have something to complain about then.

I talked on the phone with Deb. She told me she wanted to do the baptism over the weekend and since it rained, she didn't. It seemed to me that she is one of the seven and I told her so. She could be because I hadn't shared this with anyone else besides Kathleen. I am not keeping it a secret from everyone, but I'm not telling everybody I know either. It would be a lot simpler if Michael would just give me the names of the seven and I could call them. I also got a few questions from her to ask Michael, and came up with some new ones of my own.

Deb said she had a smile on her face when she called me. She said, "I feel like a kid in a candy store who can have anything I want and I don't know where to start."

I told her, "Maybe that is how we are all really supposed to feel. Wouldn't it be great if everyone could go through life like a child? Being innocent and filled with amazement as children are?"

"What is it you would ask?" Michael said to me from behind, looking over my shoulder at what I was writing.

I was startled by the way he had chosen to show up and I jumped a little to my left. "Don't do that Michael. You could give a man a heart attack sneaking up on him that way. Couldn't you just appear in front of me from now on so I know you are coming?" I requested. "I have some more questions for you from Donna," I said.

"Tell Donna she worries as if worrying brings value. Did I not tell you riches would be set upon you and yours? When it is time for you to take up that which is yours and cross the land to your new home, I will see that you are supplied with means to do so. Those whom she calls the children will live the life they are meant to. She would do well to believe with all her heart and trust that not only are they in

your care, but in God's care also. God has guaranteed a place of prominence on earth and in heaven. She shall not want for herself or the children. Know you of all this, wife of God's servant, and your headache will be gone. Guide your husband in matters of money for he cares little for it. A fool he is not. Yet he would lose it all if left alone. Your job in life is to guard him from himself."

"Deb wanted to know how she could serve God and see that children are cared for and nurtured. What I think she really wants to know is what is her purpose in all this."

"She knows as well as you that she is one of the seven. Act not that this is a mystery to you or her. Had she not heard the call she would not have to ask. Your third master is with you. Deb will be known as the one who brings light

to the souls of children. She will lift the loads
that have been placed on them so they may
play as a child was meant to do. She will learn
what you teach and take it into the world so
that a child will hear."

"What do you mean, third master? I count
only two unless you mean Donna. Is she one of
the seven and I just didn't see it?" I questioned.

**"Donna is not one of the seven you will
teach. She is a master in her own right and it
would do you well to listen to her counsel."**

Someone came to my mind as to who it might
be. "I'll give him a call and see what happens,"
I said to myself.

Deb asked a friend of hers, "If you could ask
God any question you wanted, what would it
be?" Her friend is having trouble with her
boyfriend's children and that's what was most

heavy on her mind.

This is not the question Deb's friend wanted me to ask Michael, but it is the one I heard. So I told Michael, "It seems that this friend lives with a divorced man. The kids are now telling her and their father that they are living in adultery. Is this so?"

"Within the laws of man, she is. However, according to God, adultery is much different. When God gave to Moses, "Thou shall not commit adultery", he gave not his permission to go whoring. If a husband or wife goes to lie down with another, this is whoring and no bricks are made. Divorce is not adultery in God's eyes. It does not please God that a man or woman stays with one who would abuse them. Abuse is the highest form of adultery and grounds for divorce. Should a man or

woman marry or live as husband and wife with one who has been divorced, this is not adultery."

"What about the other commandments? What are they saying?" I questioned.

"The only commandment that humanity should concern itself with is the one Jesus has given, 'love one another as I have loved you.'"

"Another thing Deb wanted to know is if I may tell the seven all that you have told me?" I added.

"You are free to tell all that I have told to you, save for the meaning of the *Book of Revelations*. This you will only tell to all seven at once, when you are gathered. They will take this teaching to the world then and not before."

"One other thing we talked about was which

will be complete first, the seven or the book?"

"The book shall you finish before the year is out. The seven shall you have before you are half a hundred in years. I tell you this of the seven so you and you alone will know."

Michael told me something about the seven. I am not putting it in now because I don't want to give anyone any ideas before we are gathered.

"What is going to happen with the religions other than Christianity? Like Islam for example, or Hinduism or Buddhism, because you haven't talked about them."

"What you will teach is for all faiths, for all have strayed from the truth. Each has had its prophets enlightening the people as to God's word. Even as Mohammed is God's prophet so are they all. When Mohammed spoke of the infidel, he was speaking of the

believers who say they believe and do not. An infidel is not outside of his own religion but infidels are in each of them. If one seeks the infidel or sinner to enlighten, I say look no further than your reflection in a pond. If you see one there, enlighten him. Should you see none there, you will see none anywhere.

"I will give a second wonder from God. If you will leave the seas unmolested for two years of your time, God will bring forth such abundance in the sea that it will feed the world till the time of change. If you do not, it is you who fish who will go hungry."

I mentioned, "Deb and I know someone who has taught a lot of people and she was wondering what will happen to the work he started?"

"His teachings will go in another direction.

**That which is now will be no more. Divine
intervention will alter the course it is on."**

"Can you be more specific?" I asked.

**"No.   What you ask, you will write or
speak of and this may change the outcome.   Go
now.   Be at peace and teach only love."**

I'm finding it harder and harder to wait until
the seven are together before I start teaching.
Questions are coming up that could be answered
if I were allowed to talk about the *Book of
Revelations*.   I think I know what is meant by,
'lead me not into temptation.'   Maybe that's
what Jesus was talking about when he said,
"Thou shalt not tempt the Lord thy God."
Better clear up what I just said so you don't get
the idea I think I'm God.   I'm not, so don't even
think for a moment I am.   What I'm saying is that
there is something in being human that allows us

to say or do something we shouldn't. If we think we have a good enough reason, we do or say it anyway. Guess this is just me complaining again because I know something I can't tell.

"Joe, you are not forbidden to tell. However, if you do, you will not be heard. The time is not now for this knowledge. Those who would hear are as green fruits and would be bitter unless they are ripened on the vine. That which is picked before it is ripe, will, no matter how long it stands, stay bitter until it rots. You would not tell a child of something that he could not understand or use until he is grown. There is growing taking place in all those you will teach. Let them grow."

"I hear what you are saying Michael and I will wait. To what do I owe this visit?" I asked.

"I come to give you the last and final word

of God. Give you this to all nations of the world. My lord God honors those who do these works and says:

Hear you my children that you may live joyously and long. War not with your brothers and sisters for they will be shown the way of peace. Fear not the mighty armies for in the time to come I will hold them at bay.

Replant the lands you have made barren with that which you have taken from it. I will give rain to the lands that have been dry that you may grow food.

I will make clean the waters that you have made unclean, as will I the air you breathe and the earth you walk on.

I will take from you disease and your misshapen bodies so you will be strong.

Know that you are loved and will be with

me for all time, for I have made a place for you.

Fear not death for you live forever with me. You are of me.

Fear not the words of those who damn you, for those who do are unenlightened.

I will call each of you into my arms and bestow the gifts of paradise upon you all. That which you have earned will be multiplied a thousand times over. That which you have given to those I have sent, though you know them not, will you receive a thousand times a thousand gifts.

My servant has written the truths for you to see. He will teach his masters but for a little time and then will teach them no more. He will send them into the world and teach other masters to teach. Hear them.

My words are done. My love is not. Blessed are you all so says 'I AM', the Lord God."

Whenever Michael is done speaking, I have to take a few moments to get myself composed again. By the time my mind was clear this time, he was gone without a word.

"Michael. Oh, Michael," I said again, but there was no answer. "Are you gone? Oh please, don't be gone. There is so much I have to ask you yet. Can you hear me? Talk to me if you can hear me, damn it. I need you to tell me --" That is when I knew Michael was gone. He could have at least said good-bye.

I felt like someone had died and I wouldn't ever see them again. I got misty even though I knew I would see him when I go home to God.

(HEY, WAIT JUST A MINUTE. What is this I

will teach for just a little? Does this mean I am going to die?).

"No, Joe, it doesn't mean you are going to die."

"Michael, I thought you were gone forever and I would never see you again," I said.

"All it means is that God has other work for you. You will not see me again until the seven are together but you will hear me in your heart. I will guide you in all that you do not know. ALL YOU NEED TO DO IS LISTEN. My time with you is done. Get that which you have written out into the world. I will be with you and the seven masters soon. Joe, one more thing -- good-bye."

Michael faded away just as he did the very first time I saw him. I know I am going to miss him in spite of the fact I will see him again. It is up to me now to get the message out to the world. I don't have a clue how I'm supposed to do this, but if you're reading this you'll know I found out.

I got a call from Deb; she said that she had been wanting to do the baptism ever since I told her about it, (of course it had to be done right). "I will go to a hill and be by myself, very spiritual," she said, "but hard to find the time with my lifestyle." Finally after a few weeks, she decided it didn't really matter how or when -- just do it!! On November 13, she set out a bowl of very good cabernet in her yard. It was difficult for her to stay quiet with two children wanting breakfast and her need to comfort her husband whose father's funeral was that afternoon. For whatever reason she did not do the baptism before, this was the day. Quietly and quickly, Deb washed her feet and hands as directed. She said the words, then poured the wine onto the ground. Deb slipped upstairs to find some quiet time in her bedroom. There she sat in meditation, waiting for some profound voice to come booming into her head. There was none, she did however have a thought that came to her, "You will be divinely guided as it is needed." "O.K.," she said to herself. "This makes sense to me. When the time comes I will know." Then she went to get ready for the service.

Then she told me this. "I stepped out of the shower and noticed the mirror had hardly any steam on it. I looked over to the small mirror on the left and noticed there was more steam reflecting on the big mirror than I had originally seen. I looked back -- no, there wasn't -- well, from the smaller mirror's perspective there was. The steam was in the shape of what looked like an oval with a small circle inside like an eye on the mirror. *No way, it's just the way the mirror was cleaned last,* I thought, *but I could not see it from a straight view in front of me, only from a side angle.* As I saw what it appeared to be I was moved deeply in my soul. I started to cry. I just stood there in appreciation, knowing that I am guided, protected and filled with love. It then faded away. I asked for assistance in listening to the guidance as it comes. Stranger things have happened," she said, referring to my own experience.

You know the more I think about it, the less I think it's strange. Throughout history and in the Bible, people have been visited by divine spirits or what we call angels. Is there any reason why a race of people would all of a sudden stop being visited? Would stop being guided or protected? Do you think God just decided one day "That's it, I have had enough; they are on their own?" Is it possible God's children stopped listening or have we just learned to ignore what we hear?

I have known Deb for about ten years and I bet I haven't spoken more than two hundred words to her. I tell her about what is happening, give her a copy of what I am writing and she takes to it like a duck takes to water. Why? Questions, so many questions and the answers, I think for now I'll let you figure them out. It's really not that hard if you stop and think about it.

This whole experience over the past year has raised a lot of questions in my mind. Take for instance what we have learned about God as we grew up. An omnipotent being with a long white beard sitting on a golden throne and dressed in white robes, just waiting for the time to judge everybody and everything. Then when the time comes, God gets to say which souls have been good enough to enter heaven. You mean to tell me that God, Who knows all, is all, can do anything God wants, would do that? Given that God is love, would God create the human race only to give a certain number of us the right to heaven? Do you think it might be that there is not enough room for everybody? Well, let's see, we have this big new house that only has so many rooms. I am going to let all my good children move in and all the bad ones; well, they can just go to hell. That would be like taking your kids out in the middle of a wilderness and dropping them off blindfolded. Yes, I know you would take off a blindfold now and then, but come on, this is still like letting them play Russian Roulette. The ones that made it back were the only ones that deserved to live? The ones that didn't make it, the bogeyman could have them? I don't think so.

Another thing that you can think about is, why would anybody think theirs is the only true religion when it is the same God that all religions are talking about? Does it really matter enough to kill one another over? Especially think about those in political power. Do you think God wants us to rule over those who believe differently from us? Have you ever read the Catholic Church's rites of excommunication? You might want to read it to see just how ridiculous a religion becomes with the power it thinks it has. It's like telling God that you have already taken care of a sinner by sending him to hell. How arrogant can anyone be to think he could damn anyone to hell? If there *were* such a place to damn someone to.

We tell children they are sinners and will go to hell from the time they're old enough to understand. We terrorize them to the point of thinking they are going to hell for the mistakes they have made. We take away any hope they have of going to heaven and leave them to think they have nothing else to lose. We make them paranoid by telling them God is watching and making a list of who is good and bad. Don't you think this sounds a bit like Santa? We fill our jails with people and even execute them for doing the things they have been programmed to do. Then to top it all off, we, "God's chosen," get to point our fingers and say, "They are evil sinners." No wonder we are in the mess we are in.

Could this be why God has given this message now? Does this mean that we are really ready to listen and do something about it? Is it possible that we have been given by God a wonderful way to live our lives? Maybe not. Maybe it has all been a dream. Maybe it's just a sugar rush I'm having from all the Pepsi I drink. Could be, but what if maybe, just maybe, it's true?

Most of you will never meet me and fewer yet will ever get to know me. That's pretty much O.K. with me because I am not all that important. The masters that God has sent me to teach will need you to be kind to them. They are alone with God's work, as will be the masters they teach. Listen to their words for they speak the truth that will bring joy to your life. Share what you hear from them with others and ask that they do the same. One of them may be the one in need who will increase your rewards a thousand times a thousand.

Don't forget to laugh at life and the things that happen in it. Don't forget to laugh at yourself, because you will find it's really very funny being you. Regardless of who you are, no one could be you better than you can. You are perfect, whole and complete just the way you are. You are made in God's image and likeness. Therefore you are all you need to be and so is everyone else. You are a child of God so act accordingly.

To me there is a real feeling of freedom in life now. Sure, I have a big job ahead of me and at times it is scary because I don't know how it will turn out. It is also exciting to know that I have been chosen to do this. At least I no longer walk around asking the questions: "What is my purpose in being here?" and "What is the meaning of life?" That is the most freeing thing of all if you stop and think about it. I need to end this book somewhere and it might as well be here. May your bricks be many. Be at peace and teach only love.

Hey, wait a minute, what does Michael mean, "God has other work for me to do?"

The Beginning...

Epilogue

It is late in December now, going on a year since I finished the book. I have neither seen nor heard from the angel Michael. I have a publisher and it looks like the book will be in print this fall.

The best part of these past months is the three masters I have found. Deb is the first, a warm and wonderful woman with a husband and two daughters. She has a way with children and not just her own. When she spends time with any child, that child goes away knowing s/he is somebody special, perfect and loved. Deb gives of herself in such a way that the child feels s/he can accomplish anything. The best thing about her is that she can teach others to do this too. I would say to anyone who would teach a child, to come sit and spend a day with her. Whatever one learns from her is more valuable than any university could hope to teach.

Then there is Mark, a man of soft spoken words and gentle of nature. His passion is in song and music. To hear him speak is like music to the ear but to hear him sing is to hear the voice of an angel in the air. More amazing than his voice is the way he interacts with people. Mark can take a moment of time to be with you, in a way that you realize maybe no one has ever truly been with you before. He really can hear what you are saying and you can really hear what he has said. After spending a day with Mark you will know that someone cares about you for who you are.

Kathleen is the most fun of the three. She bubbles with excitement and a joy which is contagious to anyone who comes in contact with her. She is one of the most emotional and honest people I know. Even though she has been ill for several years you would not know it by the way she acts. Kathleen can heal the emotions to free the spirit in ways no other person, that I have seen, can do. Time with her is well spent given the grace God has bestowed upon her.

The three of them have been a great comfort to me. I have been able to speak to them about things few people are capable of understanding. I sometimes wonder how many people out there can hear and understand. Michael has told me I will gather the seven Masters over the next two years. He also said I would have them gathered before I am a half century old. I look for them in the people I know and have known and yet have only found three. Maybe someone will read this book and know they are one of the seven. If this happens for you, write me in care of the publisher. You well may be one or one that the seven will teach. As I teach the Masters I will write down what is given to them and put it in the next book. I think it is important that this teaching gets to the world also. Each of the Masters has a unique gift or talent to reach someone in a special way. I will tell what gift they have so you can seek them out. Learn from them in the manner they teach, that which you need to know.

I have told my wife and the three Masters of a sign of something wonderful about to happen. Two signs have already happened and when the last occurs, we will know it has been set in motion. I have told no others of this because I do not wish to cause it by what I have said.

Blessings, Gifts & Deeds

"I find *Blessings, Gifts & Deeds* to be transformative and uplifting. I have enjoyed reading it and have shared it with friends. I know this heartening and grounding book has an audience out there waiting for it."

-Andrew Ramer

Andrew Ramer is the author of:
Angel Answers, A Joyful Guide To Creating Heaven On Earth.

And has co-authored:
Ask Your Angels, with Alma Daniel,
as well as several other books on spiritual dimensions.

Noteworthy

Blessings, Gifts & Deeds

_____

_____

_____

_____

_____

_____

_____

_____

_____

_____

_____

_____

Noteworthy

Blessings, Gifts & Deeds

_____

_____

_____

_____

_____

_____

_____

_____

_____

_____

_____

Noteworthy

Blessings, Gifts & Deeds

_____

_____

_____

_____

_____

_____

_____

_____

_____

_____

_____

Noteworthy

Blessings, Gifts & Deeds

_____

_____

_____

_____

_____

_____

_____

_____

_____

_____

_____

_____

Noteworthy

Blessings, Gifts & Deeds

Noteworthy

Blessings, Gifts & Deeds

_____

_____

_____

_____

_____

_____

_____

_____

_____

_____

_____

Noteworthy

Blessings, Gifts & Deeds